THIS L LIGHT

A POETIC BOOK OF CHRISTIAN INSPIRATION ABOUT LOVE, ENCOURAGEMENT AND THE TRIALS OF LIFE

JUNE ALEXIS JOHNSON-FERRELL

outskirtspress
DENVER, COLORADO

This book of poetry is dedicated first to my Lord and Savior
Jesus Christ who is the head of my life and in loving memory
and tribute to my father, the late Alexander Mangrum
who always said to HOLD ON and to my brother, the late,
Stanley Alexander Mangrum who believed in me and said
that I could do this book. They were two remarkable and
wonderful men. It is also dedicated to my children
Troy, Tara and Carrie.

CONTENTS

ACKNOWLEDGEMENTS

I thank my wonderful family and friends. I have been truly blessed with those here and those who have gone to be with the Lord. I give special thanks to my recently deceased father, Alexander Mangrum, a wonderful man who was the Great Encourager and eternal optimist. He encouraged us to always strive to be the best, do your best and do what is right. Be a leader not a follower and to HOLD ON and Trust in GOD. He was a wise and positive person and a wonderful example of a Christian man who with my mother, Mary raised my siblings and I to be God fearing and to love the Lord. Most importantly I thank God and my Lord and Savior Jesus Christ for giving me the ideas for this book and allowing me to do this.

I also thank my late and great brother, Stanley Alexander Mangrum who also recently passed away. He encouraged me to write a book and had confidence in me that I could do it when I didn't. He was a kind and thoughtful man. He was the best brother that any sister could ever have and one of the nicest men I have ever known.

I also thank my beautiful and loving mom, Mary Annette Mangrum who died many years ago when I was 16 years old, but gave my siblings and myself a wonderful start in life. I was also blessed with a wonderful sister, Barbara Elaine Andrews who has also been deceased for many years, and my baby brother, Kenneth Michael Mangrum who died at the age of 15 years old many years ago, and who was also very special. They were all remarkable people and I feel so blessed to have been born into my family. I also acknowledge my sister, Landria Kim Jeffries.

I thank my family members on both sides of my family. All of my cousins who have been with me through trials, tribulations and moments of joy and celebration to console, love, support and encourage me. All that you have done for me is truly appreciated. I also thank my deceased grandparents on both sides of my family and aunts, uncles and cousins who were always so supportive.

I thank my sister in Christ, Val Randle, a gifted published poet who was kind enough to give me pointers with regard to doing this book of poetry and was so positive and helpful. Special thanks to Betty Jenkins, a true Christian woman and my Zion Chapel Baptist Church Family. Thanks to Kristi Copez of my Smooth Cha Cha's ballroom dance group for your encouragement and support.

I thank my lifelong friend, Patricia Daniels who has been like a sister and all of our late night phone conversations over the years to encourage, uplift and support each other. Also thanks to my Sister-in-Laws who really are like sisters. You know who you are. I love and appreciate you. I thank the publisher of this book and their staff for assisting me in this process. It has been truly appreciated and I thank them for their outstanding work in doing such a fantastic job to help make this book a reality.

I also thank and acknowledge my children, Troy McQueen, Tara Johnson and Carrie Johnson for your love and support and my daughter-in-law and grandchildren of whom I am all very proud. I also acknowledge my many nieces and nephews, I am proud to be your aunt. Also special thanks to Gary Leif of Leif Photography in Roseburg, Oregon for allowing me to use your beautiful photo for the cover of this book.

INTRODUCTION

I have been writing poetry off and on for many years. However over the years I worked, married, divorced was a single mom, and raised three children with God's help and assistance from their fathers, family and friends. I was blessed with many jobs over the years, and supported my family. I observed the trials and tribulations of others as a Social Worker and tried to help when I could. I attended college full time as an adult while working full time, while my children were in junior high school. Later in life I was my father's guardian for eight years. I've experienced or observed joy, peace, happiness, trials, tribulations, disappointments, betrayal, heartbreak and promotion. I've made good choices and bad, and had to suffer the consequences. However through it all I never gave up. I was raised in a Christian home to be God fearing, to love, honor, praise and trust the Lord and to always HOLD ON. Because of this I hung in there, though sometimes feeling like giving up. I persevered. My faith and belief in God kept me going. The Lord Jesus has been with me through it all and the Holy Spirit has guided me. I am a survivor. These circumstances and situations have helped me to be more understanding, kind, loving, empathetic, and thoughtful of others. They have shaped me into a more compassionate and more non-judgmental person. God has used these circumstances and trials to make me a better person. These experiences have refined me and made me into the person that I am today. I am a work in progress. I realize that no one on this earth is perfect. The Lord says anyone on earth that believes that he or she is without sin deceives himself and makes God a liar. (Holy Bible 1 John, Chapter 1 vs., 8-10). However we as Christians although not perfect must continue to strive for excellence, although we may fall short. Through our trials and tribulations we must remember that God is with us and will carry us through if we just don't give up. We may stumble and fall but don't stay down. We all have missions in life that God has assigned us to do. We need to complete them to the best of our ability. One of my late dad's favorite sayings was, "I shall pass through this world but once. Any good therefore that I can do or any kindness that I can show to any human being let me not defer it or neglect it for I shall not pass this way again." We were not placed here only for ourselves. The poems in this book express things that I have learned, experienced or observed in my life or the lives of others. It is my hope that some of these poems will inspire, encourage or enlighten you. Some may express similar emotions or feelings that you may have experienced. When I describe a family or a Christian man or woman through poetry, this does not always reflect many families or people. However these poems express what the ideal Christian family, woman or man should look like from God's perspective, and therefore something to strive for.

You may feel sometimes that you can't make it. However, faith, trust in God and belief will take you where God wants you to go which is always for our best. Just don't give up. Stay positive and keep a good attitude. God is watching and testing our faith. Hang on in there. Rewards are ahead if we just don't give up. Always listen to the still small voice inside. It is always our guide. Think good thoughts do good deeds. Remember there are consequences for every action. Always strive for excellence. Be important but never too important to be nice. Remember in the end, we answer to God not man AND IS THERE ANYTHING TOO HARD FOR GOD.

This book is a little light that I hope will be a positive one in your life after reading it. It expresses many biblical teachings in poetic form. It is a testament to the fact that you can make it if you maintain your faith and belief in the Lord Jesus. It is my testimony of how good God has been to me and how he has blessed and carried me through every situation, good or bad that I have endured and survived. Nothing is too hard for God. I am not always in control of my life but the Lord God ultimately always is. Show humility, treat all people with respect be generous and kind. Be tolerant of the flaws in others as we all have them. Don't look down on anyone or ever give that impression. Be the light to others that you hope to see. Regardless of your circumstances in life do what is right and keep a good attitude (God is watching you). When you make a mistake ask God to forgive you and anyone you may have offended if possible, and forgive yourself and move on. When others make a mistake forgive them as well and move on. Remember the best is yet to come! Just have faith, believe, trust and hold on. Read and it is my hope that you will enjoy!

A FRIEND ALWAYS

Once upon a time, I thought I was alone. But I never was - You were always there. To lift me up when I was down. To carry me over the troubled waters—. I was not weary though things were dreary. I had faith - and remained in place, till the storms passed on by — Who was my friend through thick and thin? MY FATHER WHO IS IN HEAVEN ———— A FRIEND ALWAYS.....................

DREAMS

Dreams are mountains - like clouds in the sky. Strive to climb a mountain ~ to reach a cloud - unreachable though they seem. With God's care and love dreams can be attained - even when it rains ~ Because behind each cloud is an iridescent, and luminous rainbow - so remember ~ even when it rains, through the pain, never stop dreaming, or believing. Dreams are the substance from which success stem, so don't be grim ~. Because when all is said and done – all that remains , that can be attained are Dreams.........................

DISAPPOINTMENTS

Life can be a series of ups and downs, oh life can shift you around. Life is composed of the highs, and the lows, just as there is turmoil in a storm, and calm when the wind does not blow. Disappointments come just before the sun rises, and makes way for some pleasant surprises. Just keep the faith, and never dismay, there is always hope for a brighter day.

CALL ON HIM

Call on him, he is always there. Call on him, he is always fair. Call on him, he will never forsake you. He'll be there to take you where faith shapes you. He is always there, no matter the day, just pray, that he give you needed strength for any length- to give you happiness in any circumstance, to give you peace, in even the least. God is always there................

PEACE

Peace is stillness within and without, a serenity of spirit one
shouldn't be without. It is the most magical of emotions as
it unerringly propels us into motion to achieve the seeming
impossibilities, no matter the calamities, to achieve the colossal no
matter how implausible. Peace within is the dream of men, far more
sought than naught. Peace you see paves the way to victory. Peace
undeniably is the key.

GOD IS MY GUIDE

God is my guide. All the while. It's his strength that cannot die. It carries me forth through strife and pain, until I no longer feel the strain. He is the wisdom that sees me through - all turbulent waters and even too - gives me rest even through the test. He is the light that buoys me in times of stress, and yet he always carries me so I might rest. God is my friend to the end. He is the light that strengthens me to fight. He is the essence of my life. With him there is no end. Without him there would be no hope, and I couldn't cope. All is possible with him, no matter how improbable. God is my guide - let me always remain by his side. With him there is no failing, even though not always smooth sailing - God is my guide all the while, never ending - Always, forever, unto heaven...............

GOD'S DIVINE PLAN FOR MAN

Man was created in God's image, a minute reflection of supreme power, the everlasting tower. Given authority to make decisions with wisdom, free choice and the ability to voice, Black , Brown, Red, White. He made us in every hue, all with hopes we would express his view. None superior or inferior all made with God's exterior. Superiority is measured in the wisdom exercised by man to implement God's plan. To hate a man or woman, for Race, Creed, Color, or National origin is certain to lead to an unfortunate fate, as we have all been made to God's taste, in his image, no matter the lineage. To judge a man for other than the content of his character is indeed a caricature of God's plan, and is a sure factor in determining the inferiority of a man, for the basis of true wisdom is fear of God, to malign a man for his image is mocking God, for are we not all his children, made in his image? God's plan for man is to love others, as we love ourselves, to treat others as we would like to be treated. Demeaning others to maintain a feeling of superiority is a sure sign of inferiority, a certain way to purgatory. God's plan is the sublime plan, which includes, Health, Wealth, Happiness, and Success. God's divine plan is made for all mankind, not for a certain few, but every hue. To enter the Kingdom of Heaven, you must first love God. To enter the kingdom of Heaven, you cannot love God, and hate his image. To enter the Kingdom of Heaven, it is very important for man to learn this lesson.

WHAT'S PRECIOUS

What's precious is how we live. What's precious is the joy we give. What's precious is that we live life with great joy not strife. What's precious is how we love with the goodness that comes from above. What's precious is that we live a life of significance. What's precious is that we make a difference. What's precious is leaving here to go to that place which is so dear. What's precious is the hope that God will say on that wonderful day - with a smile, well done my child, now come rest with me for eternity.

GOD'S HEAVEN

Heaven has streets paved with gold. Heaven has flowers almost too beautiful to behold. Heaven is a place of everlasting serenity, where believers dwell for eternity. Heaven a place with God's glorious love abounding, a place where God's love is constantly astounding. Heaven, a place where hate and fear are not permitted. Heaven, a place where anger is non-existent. Heaven, a place of beautiful rainbows of radiant colors, proof that Heaven, is a place like no other. Heaven, a place of peace and joy. Heaven, a place that believers can explore. Heaven, where life goes into infinity, a place where death is not an entity. Heaven is God's reward for the believer, the sacred sanctuary of our Savior.

GOD'S WILL

Implementing God's will in your life, guarantees assistance, and protection from all strife, assures us success each day in every way. How wonderful to obtain the favor of the Savior. God's love is kind never blind. God's love is generous, never timorous. God's love is never condescending, and always undiscriminating. God's will is always for our best, and assures of success. God's love upholds us through the storms of life, and his wisdom guides us through all tensions. God's love guides us to happiness, and lifts us up from all weariness. God's love is all knowing, ever flowing - proof of his love abounding, and constantly astounding. God's love is all powerful, the everlasting tower. His love provides endless scope for all of our hopes. God is our best friend unto eternity, our friend with all sincerity. Through the good and the sad, it's never too bad for God to intervene, and correct the scene, reshape the mold, and make us whole. His power a tower, his consultation an exultation. God's love magnanimous, never calamitous. Praise be to God who is above, within, without, all about, thanks be to God for his everlasting love, for his blessings, and for his lessons from above.

DEAR SOLDIER

Dear Soldier, as you march into battle, don't forget to pray. Ask for God's presence to enter your life today. He will be with you through all strife, only he is the protector of your life. As bombs fall and rockets explode - trust that his loving arms around you will enfold. Fear not for he loves you as only God can, he'll never forsake you, he'll protect you and hold you in his hand. Though no fault of your own you've been cast into this fight. Trust the Lord he will be your light. Your body is a shell which encases your soul - when God is with you the soul always remains whole. Your soul never dies, it just goes on a flight - to be with the Lord in all his might. So whether your soul remains here as life is so dear - or departs on a flight to be with God in all of his might - Just remember Dear Soldier, your country loves you much, all of our hearts you have touched. Please trust in the Lord with all your heart - be of good courage - his love will never depart. Though you stand in the fiery furnace this day, be of good cheer - KNOW THAT GOD IS ALWAYS NEAR.

DESTINY

Within your heart is your destiny, made unto eternity. The pattern of your thoughts are not for naught, they determine the tide - how it may ride, up the ladder of success, or ever regressing to the depths. It's up to you, how the tide turns~ so be ever vigilant to image the best as this will be the test of your success. The good seeds you plant are synonymous with happiness, the good thoughts you project are steps ever leading the way to a brighter day. This is the only way to achieve that many splendored day. It is in this respect that we must pay our dues. Good thinking is an attribute with which very few of us are naturally imbued. Therefore, vigilance in governing our thoughts is required, for us to go higher. Good deeds have wings that soar the heights, unto beautiful flight. Beware, yet dare - think the thoughts, do the deeds that do please, as God would have it to be, and one day they will produce a great and happy Destiny.

MY GOD

My God is mighty, awesome, good and worthy to be praised. He is the Alpha and Omega to all my days. He lifts me up when I am down. He sets my feet on solid ground. The Lord sits high and looks low. He's all over and everywhere we know. We can count on him if we dare for he is fair and always cares. Cast your worries on Christ Jesus for he will never leave us. I love him so and make sure he knows. He's carried me all along the way as long as I remember to pray. There is no battle too great no worry too small. The Lord Jesus is there to cover it all. My God is awesome, there is no reason to fear the season. I can't thank God enough for his blessings and for helping me to pass the testing. I thank God for his grace, mercy and love which is astounding and constantly abounding that comes from above.

HOLD ON

Hold on to God's hand. Hold on and trust in his plan. Hold on, God is with you. He will always be there to uplift you. Hold on when things go wrong. Just as life is like a song with a melody that is strong. Always remember that God is there holding you in his arms. We may fall but remember that God is over all. He'll be there to break the fall. Our tribulations are chances for us to experience his miracles, an opportunity for God to catapult us to the pinnacle. Don't despair. He is truly there, always around us, within and about us. Almighty God dispensing his love straight from above. Our dreams will unfold but we must remember to hold. God loves us and cares and guides us through all snares. He expects us to hold on and trust, and to always remember that He truly loves us!

HOPE

You are so kind, it's been a long time. I never knew life could be so good. It's been quite sad to never have had such a love - but that was. Today I'm glad for the love that has been sent my way~. Thank you Lord, Oh, what a day! My love is here to stay. It's so great on this date, to have met such a kind and wonderful mate. Thank you for life - Thank you for right, and even strife. I'm so glad for this love sent from above. Thanks for the intervention of your divine hand, for you had a great plan. It's no mystery the wizardry of what God can do, so I wasn't blue. Thank you Lord for I know it was in your plan - the pains were for gain, the rain the same. The sun is now shining, and I'm climbing the heights, to see the beautiful sights. Thank you Lord! For I'm finally on my way amidst a new and sunshiny day!

OVERCOME SADNESS

Overcome sadness, get up get moving. God will help you start if you just do your part. Be happy today. It is a decision that you must make. Find something positive to do then you won't be blue. God will help you but you must not loose heart, just trust in the Lord and do your part. Talk to a friend, give them a grin -encourage them so that they are not grim. Lend a helping hand to your fellow man. Take a walk, exercise and you will exorcize those negative thoughts that lead to naught, and come what may don't forget to pray. Depression is temporary, refuse to let it become stationary. Develop an action plan today, put it into play. Enjoy life's meaningful pleasures. In our Savior's eyes we are his treasures. Put your trust in Jesus, he will never leave us.

FRIENDSHIP

A friend is there through thick and thin, even if you don't win. A confidante and ally in strife, a companion in the joys and sorrows that compose life. A person who is kind and true as well as honest with you. Who will lift your spirits when you are feeling blue. Who will sacrifice to help elevate you in life. When your dreams are fulfilled is when they are most thrilled. A friend is there no matter what - To have such a person, Oh! what luck.

HAPPINESS

Happiness is a feeling of peace, never the least. It's a serenity which is an entity. A joy in the pleasures of life which never cause strife. A delightful smile never exhibiting guile, a wisdom that's ever available, never saleable. Joy in the delight of others which is always sincere, never a veneer. Willingness to help others to achieve their dreams, no matter the team. Giving freely, never greedy, always uplifting, never deprecating. The sum total of these qualities a rarity, never leading to disparity. Transcending the mediocre to build an aura of kindness, without strife, love which is not selfish. Happiness, the sum total of real success, the gift of which we are all in quest. God's reward for a life well lived, a job well done, giving us the ability to touch the Sun.................

WHO'S IMPORTANT?

Who's important? All of us are important in God's eyes. He considers us all a great prize. Importance is measured by God in how well each of us complete our missions that he has assigned and designed . We all have a job to do in the life that God has allowed you. It's not measured by your career, position, degree or pedigree. Importance is measured by God in how well we complete the task he has assigned. How well we recognize him in its' design. Importance is measured by being and doing your best, never less and completing the task. Completing the task at hand as God has a great plan. Your importance is determined by how well you complete your duties and honor God truly, with a good attitude, gratitude and a sense of servitude. Be humble and kind, keep this in mind as these are the ways that God measures your days and importance and determines your fortunes.

WHERE YOU ARE

To the man of my dreams, a faceless image in a dream, I always yearned for you - now I've found you. I'm afraid within, oh is it a sin to be so grateful within. Once upon a time, I thought I would never find you, but the time has come nigh, I'm on a high, just for the love of you. The light in your eyes ~ the curve of your smile, the sound of your laughter, is all I need, can't you see, being by your side is where I always want to be. Through the worst of times ~ Through the best of times~, To comfort you, and love you, be near you never weary of you. Where you are is where I always want to be———.

MEMORIES

I miss you, and when all is said and done - I love you, and always will ~ But - I must let go - move on ~ When I'm all alone - I'll think of you in passing ~ But it wasn't meant to be - no - no- no, but oh in my dreams you'll always be ~ your smile, your eyes, your face, your arms around me ~. Memories - nothing can take those away from me.

DOUBT

Sometimes we wait and wonder if God knows our pain. When he's coming to relieve the strain. When is the break through that we expect as we wait in righteousness. Don't give up - God hears your prayers. He will answer in a way that's best for you, just hang in there he will see you through. The battle may be almost won, if you give up you will never touch the sun. You must ask, trust, believe and don't doubt. The Lord Jesus will soon bring you out.

YOUNG LADIES (BE A LADY)

Young ladies be soft spoken, modest and kind. Remember the good that is coming to you takes time. Carry yourself with dignity, and integrity. Exhibit character, grace and moral clarity. Respect others and watch your behavior and be a credit to our Savior. Remain morally strong and don't do wrong. Refrain from promiscuity as it will follow you into perpetuity. Don't let your reputation demean you, show the goodness that is in you. Show quality in what you say and do. You are a child of the most high God and must remain true. Carry yourself in this way and make sure that you pray. Honor the Lord Jesus in all that you do. He'll bless you with the right man in time when due. Just don't rush it as the Lord only wants good for you. Be a lady daily, don't be loud, make your family proud. In time the Lord will bless you in such a mighty way, that you will be glad that you did wait and pray.

GOODBYE

Life with its twists, and turns, who would have ever thought it wouldn't work, but our love did come to a lurch. Oh how I yearn for you, to be able to turn to you. Will I ever be free of this yen but even then, I will always remember ~ There's no joy without some pain, it's all one and the same. My love for you will never end - Even when we meet by chance I will never forget our romance - I'll smile at you - and walk away, but my heart will always say I love you, and yearn for your touch, for it meant so much ~. But, I must never let you know - so I'll lift my chin - step on with a grin, but inside I'll cry, for my love will never die. Goodbye my love, for I did try - Goodbye.............

FLOWER PETALS OF LIFE

Have you ever noticed how a flower petal unfolds? That's the way life goes. Have you ever noticed how dreams do come true? Just trust in God he will see you through. He knows the plan as you must know, he has mapped the road as we go. He's aware of your dreams, and desires in your quest to reach higher. Heeding not his voice in a choice produces disastrous consequences in every circumstance. He has seen the dreams of many fold, the results of not listening taking its toll. The secret of success is following the path which God has mapped. It's heeding his call no matter the rest. It's persevering never veering. It's heeding the still small voice inside, our never erring guide. Just trust in him, you'll not go wrong. Just trust in him and it won't be long - before you see your dreams unfold, no matter what the bell tolls. Plant your seeds with your deeds. Water your plants with love, kindness, honesty, and integrity, and at harvest time you will not be lacking. Your dreams will unfold in ways so marvelous that they could only be described as superfluous. The flower petals of life are indeed a miracle, propelling us to the pinnacle. Success does not elude you, it chooses you. Just live the life that God has planned, and your dreams will come true, in every hue, ESPECIALLY FOR YOU....................

WHAT IS FAMILY?

Family, a safe haven for us, composed of people we trust. Family a source of support and hopefully a place of great rapport. Ups and downs, they come around, but family is always there to share and care. A family consist of those we love, those special people sent from above. Family is a source of comfort in time of sorrow, helping us to pull things together in the hopes of a brighter tomorrow. Family, helping us to celebrate our joy, who could ask for more. Family the team that encourages our dreams, no matter how dismal things seem. Family is composed of those who care, no matter what, who love us whether we're good or not. God designed family especially for us you know, to nurture us as we grow. Family fills a need, enabling us to succeed. With families such as these, yes God is greatly pleased!

VICTORY

When you feel sad, just trust in the Lord he will make you glad. Trust him in the good times. Trust him in the bad. He'll be there to carry you along the way - just pray. He's a miracle maker, our Savior. His power a tower, his presence magnificent. When you are feeling blue just trust in Jesus he will see you through. Though the storms of life will toss you around, trusting in the Lord Jesus will bring events into your life that will astound. Victory is at hand if you just stand, when you have done all that you can. God's will for your life is marvelous, your destiny superfluous. The Lord Jesus will hold you in his hand if you just hold on and trust in his plan. The battle will be won by the Lord Jesus don't doubt, whom you could not do without. Trust him with all of your might. All praises go to the King of Kings, the Creator of the universe who is in command and has all power in his hands!

AWESOME GOD

When all seems lost and the pain is unbearable. Remember that
our God is the repairer. He fixes what's broken and gives us his
love as a token. We are marvelous in his eyes and he considers us
a great prize. He made us to live, love and die, and not to lie. He
expects that we live a life of service and integrity before we enter into
eternity. To travel the road that he has planned and to remember
in finality we do not answer to man. To complete our mission in
honesty and truth. To remain in submission to his will which he
makes clear. His power a tower, his consultation an exultation. His
will real. His wisdom unending, his magnificence transcending.
The almighty God the Creator of the universe and us. Our guide,
director and protector, magnificent, mighty, awesome God.

MISTAKES

In spite of all the mistakes that I made, God was never far away. I turned to him and he turned to me. He lifted me up so that I could see. He gave me strength for any length. He comforted me when I felt alone and helped me to move on. He forgave me and helped keep me strong. I read my bible and I prayed. I did not stray. He led me along the way so that I could see another day. God is my boss. I love him so much for his son Jesus died, rose again and paid the cost on the cross so I would not be lost. Turn to Jesus when you pray, in the hopes of a brighter day. Don't give up - Great things are ahead for you. JUST TRUST AND HOLD ON, and don't be sad, be glad, for God will bless you with wonders that you never had!

GRATEFUL

Thank you Lord for all that you have done, without you I would be no one. Thanks for the gift of your son, Lord Jesus that if we accept him and repent of sin, - we might live on. Thanks for your goodness, mercy, grace and love sent to us straight from above. Thanks for your guidance and wisdom to help us live on, in the hopes of one day seeing your son. Thanks for your answering prayers with your divine wisdom, helping us to be in concert with your vision. Thanks for being there and knowing that you care. Thanks for the course that we must run in our efforts to touch the sun. Thanks for the trials to refine us like gold to form character that is great to behold. Thanks for life, health, family and friends to the end. I can't thank you enough for how good you have been. Thank you!

A CHRISTIAN'S LIFE

A Christian's life is not always smooth. We are sometimes bombarded with situations that devastate us through and through. Just trust in the Lord he will see to you. Never give up, it's just a test, endure in righteousness . He promises us a future of success and not of pain if we keep our trust in him and survive the strain. Just hold on to his hand, and trust him to complete his plan. There's sunshine at the end of the rainbow you know, so remain steadfast in your faith. God will bless you greatly if you just stand in place. No matter the length or circumstance God will bless you with a break through that only he could do, outcomes so miraculous you are no longer blue. Dreams fulfilled that are surreal. Just trust in him through the pain and the rain. Remember that God loves you and is holding you in the palm of his hand!

CHERISH

Cherish those you love. Show them Christ Jesus in your behavior to remind them of the Savior. Life is passing us by each day. Make time to pray. Be happy and the light that brightens someone's day. A cheery word, a thoughtful deed, a smile, a warm embrace. These are actions that will place a smile on someone's face. A motivator that we can still run this race. The enemy wants to bring us down, but God is all around. Our heavenly father makes earthly angels of us to encourage others and to pray, to keep the devil at bay for those who are saved. So joyfully move on to another day with faith in God's grace. All of us want to be valued and loved. To be granted grace and mercy in receiving from above. Show those you love God's grace. By actions and in deeds be pleasing to our heavenly Father who provides for all of our needs.

DON'T FORGET YOUR FAMILY

Never forget your family when you achieve success. Don't forget your family who helped you through stress. Those who loved you regardless. Don't forget those who started you on your way, who urged you to pray. Don't forget those who taught you right from wrong and to remain strong. Who dried your tears and calmed your fears. Don't forget those who supported you through life's test and encouraged you when you were not at your best. Don't forget those who provided for you and guided you, who fought for you through all test. Who tried to protect you though not always with success. Who picked you up when you were down and tried to help you to turn it around. Who coaxed you up so that you might fight, realizing that God was your light. Never forget those who encouraged you to seek God's light that you might do right. Appreciate how blessed you've been and don't forget to express this to them!

FORGIVE

Forgive so that you can live. Harboring anger, hurt and strife can only lead to a miserable life. It hinders God's blessings to you and blinds you to God's lessons. Each trial a test of our faith, a path to take us to a better place. Forgive to maintain your health, physically, mentally and emotionally, forgive totally. Forgiveness is a mandate from our Creator above, a testament to God's love. If we don't forgive others, God won't forgive us and that certainly would be tough.

MY BROTHER

(dedicated in loving memory and in tribute to my brother, the late, Mr. Stanley Alexander Mangrum, One in a million)

My brother, kind friend, loving to the end. Sympathetic, thoughtful, quiet spoken and humble, willing to help others not stumble. Gifts of the holy spirit, no limit. He loved the Lord dearly, striving to achieve victory. Good heart and smart. Humorous, supportive, patriotic and never vitriolic. Good soldier of life and Christ. Beautiful spirit, long suffering and kind no evil on his mind. Good soldier of life who shunned strife. A great brother like no other. Beautiful, kind brother, a wonderful spirit, who was just magnificent!

MY DAD

(Dedicated in loving memory and in tribute to my dad the late, Mr. Alexander Mangrum, a truly great man)

My Dad, encouraging and wise, no guile. A man of great wisdom who would listen. Supportive, genuine and kind. He was a man who spoke his mind, diplomatically not dramatically. A Christian man of dignity and character, no caricature. An encourager of all , no matter the fall. An optimist of the very highest kind, no matter the climb. Forgiving of others flaws, he was cognizant of God's laws. Fun to spend time with, it was such a gift. His personality gave others such a lift. A lover of people, hospitality no end. He was indeed a friend, and a disciple of Jesus to the end!

HEARTBROKEN

When your heart is shattered, trust in Jesus that is all that matters. God offers comfort to the broken hearted. He will help you to get started. When you are disappointed remember that you are still anointed. Enjoy each day as if your last. Trust and be faithful and stay on task. God will continue to fight for you until the last. The victory is yours so remain steadfast!!

HONOR YOUR PARENTS

Honor and respect your parents, this is one of God's Commandments. If you do this you add days to your life. If you don't you shorten your life and go to the land of the darkness in all its' starkness. Watch your mouth and your behavior, Jesus is what it's all about so please our Savior. Check your pride and ego, and don't do what's evil. Leave it at the door as God wants to bless you so much more. Do what's right and God will shower you with blessings if you just past the testing. With blessings you will live to savor as you honor our Savior. Honor and respect your parents, whether young children or adult children it doesn't matter, this commandment applies forever.

PARENTS, DO YOUR JOB

Being a parent is sometimes hard. It's not about being your child's best friend. It's about teaching, guiding, correcting and protecting them so in the end, they're trained to win. Remember parenting is a job that God allowed you. Follow it diligently through and in the end God will bless you. Sometimes the job is not pleasant as we have to deal with our children's temperament. However stay the course, stand firm and hold on. Start when your children are young. Temper love, kindness and guidance with firmness and discipline and pray for guidance and wisdom. Teach them right from wrong, and to be morally strong. Correct them when they need it so as they grow old they will not deviate. When your children grow older they will appreciate your diligence in seeing that they could live a life of significance. Being a parent is not always easy but our goal is to please The Lord Jesus.

THANK YOU

Thank you are two simple words. Together most powerful verbs. They take only a moment to say but they go a very long way. They indicate an appreciation for, admiration, celebration, kindness, and consolation. A recognition of a person's thoughtfulness that's too often ignored in thoughtlessness. These two words expressed to show our Christlikeness and attest to our excellence. Make a special point to say thank you for the big or the small, acknowledge it all. It shows humility and civility. Give others the same courtesies that you expect and you will be blessed. This causes God to smile on his child and inspires showers of blessings from heaven.

DEPRESSION

Every negative and depressing thought most often leads to naught. The devil is behind it and designed it as a pitfall for you so don't be blue, rebuke it as the lie that it is . God is keeping you in righteousness. Cast out that thought as it leads to naught. God loves you more than you know. He has great things in store for you, as you go. Just keep hold to his hand. He has a great plan. It doesn't matter how things appear today. God is clearing the way. He's doing great things in your life that you cannot see but in due, you will see too. Cast those negative and depressing thoughts out, look up and smile and don't doubt. No matter what you are going through, no matter what happened to you, trust not what you view. Trust and believe in what God can do!

CHRISTIANS, MAKING DECISIONS

When making decisions, ask God for his vision. Listen to the still small voice inside. It is your guide. He will answer yes, no or wait. He determines our fate. If you hear no voice, make no choice. Wait until the answer is clear, and you know his will. This prevents mistakes that we need not make. The answer whatever God's will infers should never deviate from his word. It should be morally and ethically correct and this is specifically what God expects. Remember the enemy is treacherous and will try to deceive us but God provides the Holy Spirit to lead us. Be sure to pay attention as a mistake can lead to contention.

A CHRISTIAN WOMAN

A Christian woman, strong, God fearing never veering. She is kind and wise always guiding her child. A Christian Woman, nurturer, chosen to prepare many for their futures. Compassionate, loving versatile and true. There is a Christian woman in every hue. As a part of God's special creations spanning many nations. She is sent straight from heaven destined to teach many lessons. Be she wife, daughter, mother or friend, it doesn't matter a Christian woman was made to win. Backbone of the home, workplace and church. Just say where she cares. A Christian woman providing that special touch which means so much. Strong but gentle, kind but firm, she is the bearer of much which is learned. Shaping the future by her example , yes a Christian woman is truly special. A Christian woman, a special creation without measure, she is a part of what God truly treasures.

A CHRISTIAN MAN

What is a Christian man? He is a man of great values, exhibiting great congeniality. He loves his fellow man and adheres to God's plan. He honors, loves and trust the Lord who guides him through all strife and is the head of his life. He is a leader who exhibits honor, integrity and is an achiever. He is a humble man, thoughtful and kind, concern for others always on his mind. A Christian man is loyal, strong and supportive, has backbone, and carries himself in a way that is royal. He is a gentleman who respects women. He loves his family, and friends and on him they can depend. He is a man to admire, someone who inspires. He is a man of courage who by his example inspires others to flourish. A Christian man fulfills God's plan, makes God proud and he smiles, as he observes his child.

ABOUT THE AUTHOR

June Alexis Johnson-Ferrell has been writing poetry off and on for many years. Because of working, being a single, divorced mom and attending college while her children were in Jr. High school she never had time to focus on her poetry. She also cared for her dad 8 years as his guardian until he passed away in 2012 at the age of 92. She worked various jobs continuously over 35+ years and retired as a Social Worker for the county of Cuyahoga in Cleveland, Ohio in 2010. Over the years she won the Editor's Choice Award in 1994, 1997 for poetry from the World of Poetry organization and was selected for inclusion into Who's Who in Poetry, Vol. III in 1989, where her biography and poem, " Destiny" was included. She also won the " Golden Poet Award," in 1989 from the World of Poetry for the poem, "Destiny." She has poems published in several poetry anthologies such as "Great Poems of The Western World , Vol. II," " Treasury of Golden Poems," "Our World's Favorite Gold and Silver Poems," "Great Poems of Our Time," and " Outstanding Poets of 1994." These were published by the National Library of Poetry and the World of Poetry. She was also selected for inclusion of her biography in" Who's Who of American Women," 2006 - 2007, and 2008-2009, and " Who's Who in the World" 30 th Edition for 2013 by the Marquis Who's Who Publication Board, and for " Who's Who In America," also for the 2013 edition by the Marquis Who's Who Publication Board. She attended college as an adult and single mom while raising her children, working full time and going to college full time. She received an Associates degree from Cuyahoga Community College, in Cleveland, Ohio and, a Bachelor's of Arts degree from Notre Dame College of Ohio in psychology in 1995, and a Master's of Arts degree from John Carroll University in Cleveland, Ohio in Counseling and Human Services in 1997. She was also licensed as a Professional Counselor in the State of Ohio. She currently resides in a suburb of Cleveland, Ohio. She has three adult children and 4 grandchildren.

She finally has time to focus on her poetic aspirations, (this book), and volunteering. (She is a mentor) She also enjoys ballroom dancing, traveling, member of her church usher board and spending time with family and friends. She attributes all of her blessings, breakthroughs, miracles, successes, and overcoming trials, tribulations, failures and adversity to the Lord and her personal Savior, Jesus Christ. She compiled this book of poetry to encourage, inspire and motivate others to know that no matter what you encounter in life, God will bring you through just don't give up. Trust him and your dreams can come true according to his perfect will for your life. She believes if God did and is doing it for her that he will do it for you. If you confess, repent and accept the Lord Jesus Christ into your life as your Lord and personal Savior, do your best, have faith, ask, trust and believe. She states that she is a walking, talking and now writing testimony of God's goodness, kindness, mercy, grace, favor and love, and through this book wants to share it with others. For more information about her see her Website at : wwwoutskirtspress.com/ThisLittleLight

CPSIA information can be obtained at www.ICGtesting.com
Printed in the USA
BVOW001922250413

319154BV00008B/235/P